Rejoice

REJOICE

MARY ANGELINE **BELL**

ISBN: 978-621-434-091-0 (softcover)
        978-621-434-092-7 (hardcover)
        978-621-434-093-4 (ebook)

Printed in New York by:

OMNIBOOK CO.
99 Wall Street, Suite 118
New York, NY 10005
USA
+1-866-216-9965
www.omnibookcompany.com

First Edition

For e-book purchase: Kindle on Amazon, Barnes and Noble
Book purchase: Amazon.com, Barnes & Noble,
and www.omnibookcompany.com

Omnibook titles may be purchased in bulk for
educational, business, fund-raising, or sales promotional use.
For more information please e-mail info@omnibookcompany.com

Designed by: Gian Carlo Tan

this book
is dedicated to

Janice Elizabeth
Jessica Rose
Jasmine Elizabeth

CONTENTS

To a Child
To the Graduate
Vital Sparkle
Thanks, Friend
It's My Brothers!
Claudia Procula
Look Now!
Great News!
We'll Celebrate!
River of Life
Waxing Waning Moon
Haiku Reverie
To Dance
On the Path
Life and Victory
Spring Blessings
What Matters
Cinquain Creatures
Contentment
The Race
Haiku Gems
Mind
Berlin
Remember the Cost
Crime Victim
Therapy
Wounded Dove
Peace
Grace
Floral Cinquains
Storm
Struggle
Choose Life
Let's Rebuild!

CHAOS AND COSMOS

Confounded, I watch
The shattered world around me
Where the creature distinguished by reason
Does constant violence to his own kind.
No sense it makes that we
Who comprehend the order of stars and atoms
Remain in inner chaos,
Causing pain and suffering,
Yet blaming only circumstance.
Yet some have found
That Order from which flows
A mighty cosmos, peace, serenity and power.
They hear the gentle whisper of tenderness and truth.

THE DREAM

I came home from my errands in the rain;
There was no one at home for me to see.
I looked for some new piece of news in vain;
You know how dull a day like this can be.
And so I fell asleep and had a dream
That I had found the place for which I hope –
A house with airy rooms where it would seem
That I could box my treasures with a rope.
At night, I'd watch the window for a star
And think of all the stars a poet can;
But then I was awakened by a car,
And I live in the noisy world of man.
Amazing how we dream and work and pay
For quietness in some unthought of way.

HARVEST

Harvest – tons of food
From the labor of only a few,
While those in the teeming cities
Labor for means of exchange
And anxiously watch the bathroom scales.
Others roam the concrete
With no labor and perhaps no dwelling.
Food stamps and food bank we have,
But is it enough while talk is cheap?
I can give a meal; I'm glad I can.
Bodies can be fed with turkeys;
Let me also help a soul to soar with eagles.

WASTED CUP

One holds an empty cup;
His thirst is great,
But no drop fills the cup.
Another's cup is full;
He has no thirst;
He pours the cup out on the ground.
Another with full cup
Drinks the sweetness,
Grateful for its comfort.
The spilled cup is wasted.
Does no one care?
Must honest thirst go yet unquenched?
Must nectar drink be spilled upon the ground?
Think now. It may be sweeter than you think
Who say you have no thirst.
The thirsty will rejoice with you
If you but drink with joy.

No cup is void of worth,
And if perchance you let the thirsty drink,
Their joy will yet rebound to you
When thirst is quenched.

SPIN

"That's the way it is," or is it?
I wasn't there; I only punched the remote.
The fanfare may be nothing;
The scorned, ignored broodling a swan.
I may know where my needle points,
But do I know a magnet?

SPRING AT LAST

I dreamed my winter frosts were at an end;
The spring had come with you; your touch and voice
Had bid my empty heart awake, rejoice,
And listen to the music love would send.
I woke and found that it was winter still;
A silence filled my heart and house as yet.
I breathed a quiet sigh of deep regret
That naught remained but the abiding chill.
When time had passed, I knew the spring was due;
The barren earth brought forth its flowers of red.
The naked trees dressed green; my nearly dead
Belief stirred with new hope the dream was true.
You came when I had learned to love and care
For shivering ones around me; spring was fair.

BRUSH STROKES

You brushed so randomly, oh hand of chance.
Or were you chance?
A firey gash was painted where
I never would have put that stroke.
I wept for the ruined work;
The brush continued.
As the sunrise glowed,
New shapes appeared
Beautiful and strong,
And I could scarcely find
The incomprehensible gash.

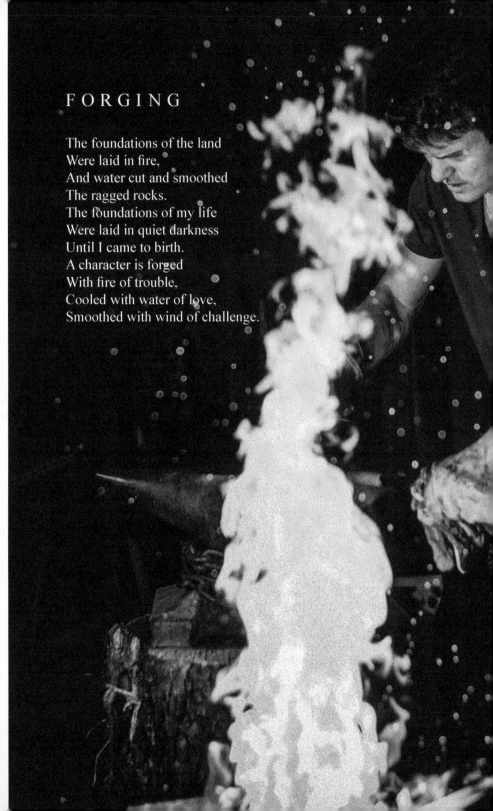

FORGING

The foundations of the land
Were laid in fire,
And water cut and smoothed
The ragged rocks.
The foundations of my life
Were laid in quiet darkness
Until I came to birth.
A character is forged
With fire of trouble,
Cooled with water of love,
Smoothed with wind of challenge.

IT IS FINISHED

Those who heard it
Thought that He Himself
Had come to naught.
The cross, the mob,
The darkness,
Then the tomb
Had sealed their broken hopes.
Then Sunday came.
He spoke and stood among them,
And they knew that death
Was finished.

APART

You were dear to me,
Though to you it meant but little.
Our lives ran separate but parallel.
Your wounds I felt. Your risks
Left me vulnerable.
Broken bonds, tears,
Achievements, hopes and dreams
Were yours and mine until
The day the window through which
I saw you
Seemed dark
And reflected the image
Of me alone.

FALSE PREMISE

Two starting paths lay at my feet;
I took the wider and the more complete.
It led past flowers, berries, trees,
And fruit for every taste to please.
But soon came brambles, thorns, and mire.
"It's but for a while," I said. The fire
of passion burned within, but then
I soon discovered this path's end.
'Twas but a cliff, a jumping o'er
into the darkness evermore.

BUILD NO WALL

Tragedies multiply;
Violence is everywhere.
Can I not build a wall?
The darkness is too much,
And some will not call evil what it is.
Why should I walk among such waste?
My light can pierce the darkness,
And if but one is guided
To the safety of love,
My walk is not in vain.

MOMENTS

Moments, like rainbows,
Fade from sight,
But not from memory.
You were there
But will not be again;
The rain is gone.
If not, I'll search for flowers,
Color them red for longing,
Green for life, blue for sighs.
There will not be another you,
But there will be rainbows.

SHARING

Sharing of tenderness is comfort;
It quenches the thirst of loneliness.
Sharing of joy is honey to the spirit;
It doubles the sweetness of weal.
Sharing of sorrow is balm for the pain;
It lights the stars in one's night.
You are the spring to my thirst,
The honey to my weal,
The stars in my sorrow,
And our love is the treasure of
Each of our moments – apart or shared.

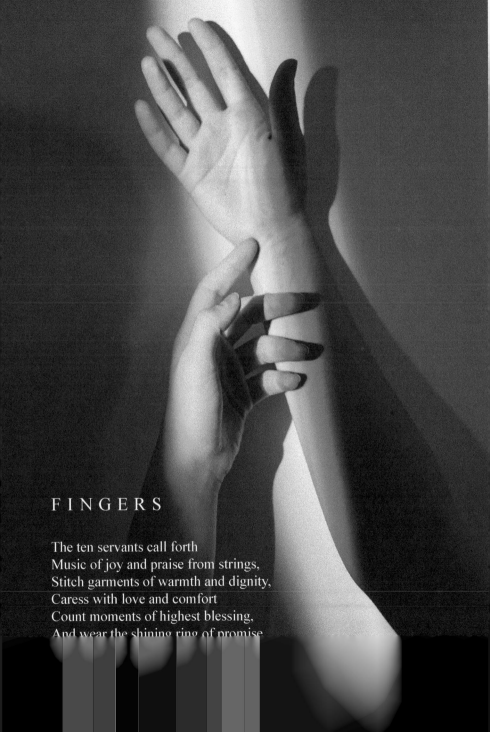

FINGERS

The ten servants call forth
Music of joy and praise from strings,
Stitch garments of warmth and dignity,
Caress with love and comfort
Count moments of highest blessing,
And wear the shining ring of promise

OK – NOT OK

I thought I was OK until
They told me I was not.
I was too tall, too short, too fat, too thin,
Or else it was the color of my skin.
My folks were poor; they came from the wrong place.
My body's flawed; I cannot win a race.
I am not learned; learning passed me by.
There's nothing in me to delight the eye.
I chose none of these states, but I was scorned until
I scorned myself and lived in anguish still.
I knew that I was not OK and then
One day I saw why I was not.
Self-centered, I had wronged my fellow man.
I held my bitterness, and from the truth I ran.
My heart was sick to death; my wretched state
Had naught to do with race or wealth or fate.
My will and mine alone had caused my pain;
Apart from God, I sought for peace in vain.
God's answer was a cross and empty tomb.
With that he healed my soul;
Now I'm OK, and you can be so too.

HAIKU HAVEN

Dark blue at evening
Soothing the long day's turmoil
As a shadow cools.

Stars of the soft night
Scattered as tiny sentries
Guarding my repose.

Glow of coming dawn
Calling me to new projects
With promise of peace.

DIFFERENT

He's different.
His life conditions didn't let him do
The things most people do,
Like have a family,
Get around as he liked,
Choose his work.
He's different.
Perhaps his body's flawed;
Perhaps his life is scarred
By happenings he did not choose,
And no one takes the time
To look upon his human heart
And no one understands.
He was different.
They knew it when they followed Him
And listened to the things He said
And watched Him deal with outcasts.
The title King seemed strange for Him.
They did not understand the cross.
He was sinless in a world of sinners.
He was different.

STILL THERE

Lord, the clouds may sometimes hide you
As they shroud the mountain peak.
Then the radar of faith
Shows your presence eternal
And my log shows the times
You have blessed me
in the splendor of sunshine,
and I await again
the vision of a shining peak.

JUDAS

It wasn't the silver I craved,
Though they expected to pay.
Like the traveler in his tent,
Weary of the journey,
I thought we should arrive.
If Jesus is indeed the King, the Christ,
Should He not prove it now?
I thought 'twould only force His hand.
I never meant for Him to die.
No sinner He, but I – I sent Him
To the cross with my wicked kiss.
I threw the cursed silver back.
With myself, what will I do?
He said that He would suffer, die,
And rise again.
Dark riddles, we thought, but then
At table He repeated it, and gave to me
The bread He dipped.
He's dead now. Did He say three days?
No, that's too long. E'en were it possible,
What could He do with me, a traitor?
He's dead now. For me it's rope,
Or wait for the third day. Waiting's
Too much agony; there's naught to gain.
Give me the rope, and let me go.

THE RAVEN BANISHED

The raven of sorrow
Flaunts his "nevermore"
To strip a soul of hope
Of any dawn from that black night.

There is a Daystar,
Sun of our hope,
Who returns to shine alone,
And darkness shall be nevermore.

SPARROW

Fragile as a fleeting breath,
Vulnerable as a tiny flower
Near treaded ground,
You flit about in sun and rain,
An object of the Father's care.
Perplexed, yet not despairing,
Hard pressed, but not yet crushed,
I walk this earth in darkness and in light
An object of the Savior's love.

THE WALL

You built a wall between us.
There it has stayed
Though I've knocked and called.
The barbed wire on top is real.
I can do nothing more of myself;
You want the wall,
But it cannot keep out
My prayers for you.

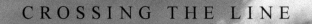

CROSSING THE LINE

Irreversible as a scar
Of anger and injustice past,
The line is firm
With all the shades of color
Leading to it.
Over there lies a harder road
With no return
And many bends,
A steep path.
There's but one way ahead
And I must take it.
Justice calls, life beckons
And I must go calmly.

DEFENDING LIFE

We are as one; we will not go away.
We will be heard, though some twist what we say.
Not 'gainst flesh and earthly ruling powers
Do we yet struggle through these midnight hours.
The soul and spirit are the focus of the strife;
Each one must choose the way of death or life.
"Where is your brother?" is God's question from of old.
Have mercy, Lord! His blood is spilled for gold.
Who is my neighbor? Is it not that one
Who, had he voice, would choose to see the sun?
Is it not she who needs a loving voice
To say the stones are stopped, and show a better choice?
We shall remain; our strength is not our own.
The dawn will come and roll away the stone.

PROMISE

As the eagle claims the sky,
So those who trust the Lord
Will claim new strength.
Wings of faith will bear them
Over mountaintops of life.
On feet of hope they will run
The race of righteousness
And walk through streets
And valleys
Surrounded by sustaining love.

CONTROL TOWER

Lord, you gave my plane
Clearance for takeoff,
Watched me on your screen,
Brought me through the stormy cloud.
I'm headed for the royal runway,
And it's comforting to know
I'm never beyond the radar
Of your love.

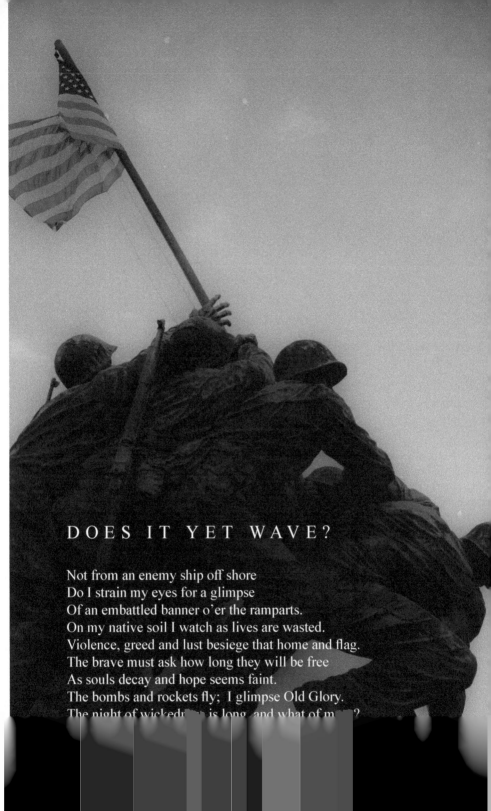

DOES IT YET WAVE?

Not from an enemy ship off shore
Do I strain my eyes for a glimpse
Of an embattled banner o'er the ramparts.
On my native soil I watch as lives are wasted.
Violence, greed and lust besiege that home and flag.
The brave must ask how long they will be free
As souls decay and hope seems faint.
The bombs and rockets fly; I glimpse Old Glory.
The night of wickedness is long, and what of me?

FORCED LANDING

The take-off was the simple spreading
Of my untried wings
And the sweet air of your presence
Bearing me to new heights.
I soared over mountains,
Through cotton clouds
And over new terrain.

Then a thundercloud struck me down
Onto strange ground.
Will I taste the sweet air of flight again?
I'll know the thundercloud by sight afar.
I want to land willingly
In a pleasant meadow
With flowers of joy
And breezes of laughter
And milk of delight.

UNATTENDED

The concert was rehearsed
For many hours
With skilled musicians.
The posters read, "Come; it's free."
The time and place was set
For music to express a love
And joy in loving.
With orchestra in place and tuned
I stepped out with baton,
But the hall was empty.
We can do no differently,
For we must play
And play we will
To those uninvited, unknown,
That it may echo in their lives
And stir again some broken chords
Where harmony had been forgotten.

CASCADES

Clear water of thought
Rushes over the rocks of memories
As its roar shuts out the city sounds
And fills the ear with itself alone.
White foam like sparks of emotion
Dances at the rocks and ripples
Into the pool of contentment,
Rippling to the end.

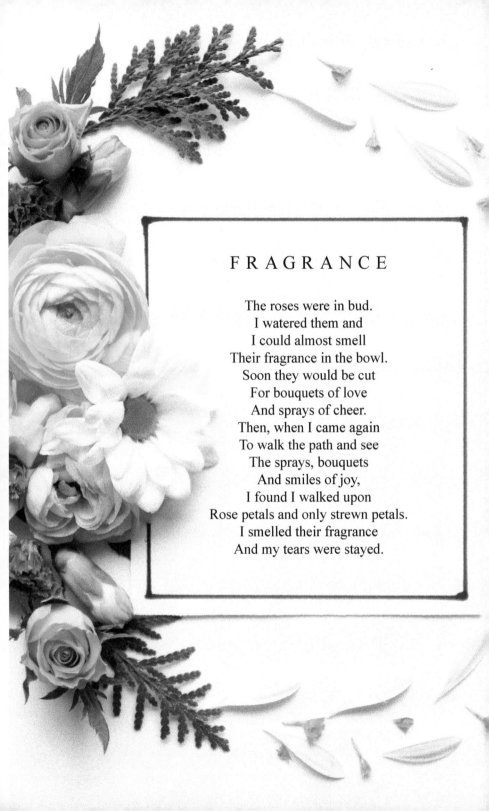

FRAGRANCE

The roses were in bud.
I watered them and
I could almost smell
Their fragrance in the bowl.
Soon they would be cut
For bouquets of love
And sprays of cheer.
Then, when I came again
To walk the path and see
The sprays, bouquets
And smiles of joy,
I found I walked upon
Rose petals and only strewn petals.
I smelled their fragrance
And my tears were stayed.

REJOICE

The grave,
So dark, so cold,
A vandalized humanity,
And nothing more makes sense.
The dawn,
The light; He lives again,
The risen Lord and King,
And those redeemed are creatures new.

Rejoice!
Go tell the world
His love revealed;
Eternal joy is ours with Him.

TO A CHILD

Soft as the kiss of a whispered breeze,
Like sunshine to a shadowed heart,
You play the sparkling moments
As an angel sings of hope and joy.
My prayers ascend to Heaven for other angels
To go before and behind you
As you meet a wretched world,
That those touched by you may be touched
By the healer, the Fount of Joy.

TO THE GRADUATE

Your talents, like stars,
Can spangle your dreams
Along with special cherished memories.

Your dreams, as your hopes,
Can show you pathways
Of knowledge, wisdom, joy and contentment.

Your journey of life
Has new adventures,
With prayers that love will go with you always.

VITAL SPARKLE

Gleaming glaciers on lofty peaks
Enchant the eyes and hold them awed.
Singing small streams in symphony
Echo in the ears and in dreams.
Refreshing rain on air and earth
Leaves scented pleasure for deep breaths.
Cold water from an ice-filled cup
Comforts the lips and tongue and throat.
Cool shower on a sweaty skin
Soothes the body and calms its stress.
Water: sea and snowflake,
Rain, river and dewdrop,
Gives life to all.

THANKS, FRIEND

My humble thanks
For being my true friend.
You saw my worth and said, "Why not?"
When I was asking several whys.
Life is a journey, and we've traveled
O'er pleasant meadows and rocky roads.

If I have made the pleasant meadows
Yet more pleasant,
And cheered you on the rocky roads,
Know you've done the same for me,
And I give thanks to God for friendship,
Showing us what we can be.

IT'S MY BROTHERS!

Joseph – next to youngest of the twelve sons of Jacob, also known as Israel. The time is between 1800 and 1700 B.C. The setting is the Middle East. Joseph is especially favored by his father because Joseph and his younger brother Benjamin were born to Rachel, who was especially loved by Jacob. One token of Jacob's favor to Joseph was a very fine coat. In all of this, and especially when Joseph told his family that he had dreamed that they were all bundling sheaves of wheat together and the other sheaves bowed down to Joseph's, his brothers resented him intensely. One day when their father sent Joseph out to where his older brothers were tending the sheep, to see whether they needed anything, the brothers stripped Joseph of his coat and threw him into a pit. When a caravan bound for Egypt came along, they pulled Joseph out of the pit and sold him as a slave. Then they dipped his coat in the blood of a slaughtered animal and took it back to their father, letting him believe that Joseph had met a gruesome death.

Twenty years later, Joseph is still in Egypt, but no longer a slave. He is an administrator next to the Pharaoh, distributing food in a time of famine. One day he is told that ten men from Canaan have come to see him. Here are his thoughts when he first sees them:

"Ten men to see me. No! Can it be? It's my brothers! They also have come for food. They don't recognize me. If they thought of me at all when they came here to Egypt, they never expected to find me in this position.

"I was really arrogant at seventeen when I strutted around in that coat which Dad gave me, and couldn't wait to tell the whole family about that dream I had. Everyone thought it was pretty transparent – that I would one day Lord it over them. Now I know what it meant. God would put me in a position to save lives, and those lives would include my own family.

"When I arrived in Egypt I was sold to a guard captain. He gave me a lot of responsibility, but then I was thrown into prison on a false accusation. I became a model prisoner, and one day two prisoners told me their dreams. God showed me that one of them would be released and restored to his former position in three days, and the other would be executed in three days. That's what happened. Then the Pharaoh himself had a disturbing dream, and the man who had been in prison with me remembered me and told the Pharaoh about me. So I was brought out of prison, and before Pharaoh, and as he told me his dream, God showed me that there would be seven years of plentiful harvest in the land, followed by seven years of severe famine. I explained this to the Pharaoh and told him that as much grain as possible should be stored during the years of plenty, so that there would then be food to distribute during the years of famine. The Pharaoh at once put me in charge of this whole project, and here I am, distributing food in time of famine.

"I haven't heard anything of the family for twenty years. My kid brother, Benjamin, is not with them. I wonder why. I've got to find out about the family, but I can't tell them who I am just yet. Somehow I've got to find out whether they have changed inside, and whether they are living with remorse about what they did to me or whether they still feel that it was good riddance. They certainly wanted to be rid of me then, but what about now?

"I can find out from them whether Dad is still alive. If he is, they'll probably mention him when I tell them I believe they are spies who have come to see and take note of what we have here and how we are doing things.

"Yes, they said their father sent them here, and they said their father had twelve sons – one is dead, and the youngest stayed at home. Well, I'll give them the grain. I'll even hide in their sacks the silver they brought to pay for the grain.

"The famine is going to last a while longer. They will probably have to return for more grain. But I'll make their seeing me conditional upon their bringing Benjamin with them. They don't like the idea; they tell me it will be very hard on our father. I understand. Benjamin and I are the only sons of his beloved Rachael, who died when Benjamin was born. But I want to see Benjamin. Perhaps if I keep one of them hostage here, Benjamin will be more likely to come with them next time. Simeon keeps saying that he will be totally answerable. Well, Simeon will be the hostage.

"They are here the second time. Very well; I will bring Simeon out to them.

"Then – I have it! They'll be staying here for a meal, and I'll have them brought to my house and seated in the order of their birth. They'll freak out when they look around at each other, because they won't know how anyone here would know their birth order.

"I sent them on their way with their grain, and I hid my own silver cup in Benjamin's sack. I sent a servant after them to tell them that I am missing my cup and they must search their sacks. The one who has the cup must stay here.

"So they've come here, very distressed because of Benjamin. They speak to me through an interpreter, but then they discuss things among themselves, not knowing that I know the language. It's getting to me. They have brought up what they did to me when they sent me to Egypt, and that much trouble has come upon them because of their brother Joseph. I am going to send everyone out of the house. I can't hold out much longer.

"Men! It's your brother Joseph. What you did to me, you meant for evil, but God meant it for good!"

CLAUDIA PROCULA

Marcus, please take this note out there to my husband. He's hearing a very difficult case this morning, but I have to communicate with him somehow. Even though Pilate is governor of this Roman province of Judea, and I am simply his wife, I have to let him know. Thank you.

I couldn't sleep until almost daylight, and then I had a most disturbing dream.

Pilate never did get along very well with Tiberius' reign, and finally he was assigned out here to Judea.

We came to Jerusalem, having heard that the Jews were a strange people with their one God and their strict laws. They resent Roman rule and Roman taxes more than any other people in the empire. But I could not stand to stay shut indoors all the time, so I got acquainted with a few of them. There was a fellow named Levi, who did a good job collecting taxes. But one day, a traveling teacher from Galilee came. I stood on the edge of the crowd of listeners. Well, it would be a different kind of world if most people really lived the things He taught. What was most intriguing, though, was his reference to a God Who is like a Father – meaning a God Who loves. How is that possible? And then one day, Levi was no longer at his usual booth taking care of his tax business. I learned that he had left the booth and gone to follow this teacher from Nazareth, called Jesus. In fact, I was told, Levi is now called Matthew and is one of Jesus' inner twelve who accompany Him everywhere.

This week Jerusalem has been crowded with visitors for the Jews' annual Passover feast. Such crowds make trouble more likely, and Pilate gets nervous then. It hasn't been easy. He has already twice angered the Jews enough that it reached the emperor's ears. If such a blunder happens again, what will happen to us? Where will we go? And Pilate usually doesn't listen to me anyway. But the man before him now is this very Jesus, brought to Pilate by their religious leaders. I don't understand. From what I've seen and heard of this Jesus, He is no political revolutionary. I even heard Him tell the temple leaders, when they asked Him, that they should render to Caesar the things that are Caesar's and to God the things that are God's. What's so dangerous about that? Yet now they're telling Pilate that Jesus is trying to make Himself a king. Even now, through these walls, I can hear the crowd shouting.

I've got to tell about my dream. I was all alone, on a dry and barren desert, and so thirsty I wasn't sure how long I would last. I kept pressing forward with what little strength I had. Then I saw someone coming toward me. I could no longer stay on my feet. I fell down spent. As I felt a hand on my shoulder and lifted my eyes, I looked up into the face of the Teacher from Galilee. Without a word, He put a cup of water to my lips, and a drink of water had never felt so good. Then I looked around, and my surroundings were no longer a desert, but a lush place of green growing things. Then I looked again into the Teacher's face. He had a look that told me I really mattered, and that's something I haven't felt for a long time, if ever. Best of all was the indescribable peace – a peace I had never known until that moment. I wanted that moment to last forever.

But then, something happened. The surroundings were barren again, and a crowd of angry men surrounded Jesus. Pilate stood next to Him, and it was to Pilate that the unruly crowd was shouting their accusations. I realized they wanted blood – nothing less would do.

I would like to believe in a just God. This Jesus has done nothing wrong. Can't Pilate at least be just? This Jesus is not violent. He can even heal the sick. He is merciful, and this world has far too little mercy.

By now, Pilate should have read my note. But, no! I hear them shouting, "Crucify!" Pilate, if this man goes to His death, the shame will be upon your head! Marcus, you say it's done, and Pilate washed his hands? That's an empty gesture. I tried to tell him; it was all I could do.

Nothing will ever be the same.

LOOK NOW!

Norman boarded the motor coach. He would have to sit beside another passenger, although he was not in the mood for conversation with a stranger. He wore his jeans and plain T-shirt and carried a small overnight bag. The distance to his home would take about an hour and a half to cover. He was glad it was no longer.

Norman took a seat beside an older man in a business suit, who had a brief case. Perhaps the man would take out something to read, and conversation would be unnecessary. But after the bus was out of downtown and onto the freeway, he turned to Norman and said, "I'm Roger Hamilton, and I have a 3-hour ride ahead of me, to Victor City. My car's in the shop, and the important meeting there would not wait. Luckily, I have friends there who will do what friends do. How about you? Going on a trip, or heading home?"

"Oh, I'm going in the direction of home," the young man replied. "My name's Norman Perry, and I grew up on the outskirts of Bennington. It's been a while since I've been there."

"So, you've lived and worked for a while in Rittenburg, which we just left?" queried Roger.

"It's not like it should have been," answered Norman after an uncomfortable hesitation. "Oh, I had good parents who would have been happy for me to take able wings and make a life of my own. Rittenburg would have been fine with them. But that's not what actually happened." Norman paused, not sure whether or

"It's a messed up world, I know," said Roger quietly. "Things don't always happen as we plan."

"No, they don't," said Norman. "You see, Mr. Hamilton, I thought I knew it all. I just wanted to be out from under any kind of rules and do what I felt like. That's what I thought adult life should be – nobody telling you what to do. I gave my parents a hard time, and one day, when I thought I had enough together, I left."

"So then what happened?" asked Roger.

"Oh, I made it to the city alright," answered Norman. "But after a while, my money ran out, and I hung out with some characters who lived mostly by robbery and extortion. We all thought we were clever enough to get away with it, but one day we got busted and ended up in the slammer. I looked at that judge and jury and realized that there was nobody in Rittenburg who cared about me. After what I had done, they were willing to pay their taxes to keep me locked up, out of sight, out of mind."

"Prison is not a pleasant place," responded Roger.

"No," answered Norman. "But it's there that some people think of things they had not thought of before. I was there for five years. It really hit me how I had blown it. None of us is made to be a self alone. We need other people and they need us. And after all that my parents had done for me, I simply kicked them in the teeth."

"So are your parents still at Bennington?" asked Roger.

"As far as I know," replied Norman. "I did not write or phone them all that time, until a week ago, just before I got out of prison. I wrote them a letter. I told them all that had happened. I told them that I had done wrong, that I knew I had blown it big time, and that I would not blame them if they wanted nothing more to do with me. I told them that I would be on this bus today. We will be able to see the place as we approach Bennington. There's an oak tree at the edge of the property. I told them that if they wanted to see me, to tie a yellow ribbon on the lowest branch of that tree, and I would get off the bus at Bennington. Then I said that if I did not see the ribbon, I would stay on the bus, go somewhere down the line, and try to look after myself." Norman paused, struggling. "It's pretty lonely when you've blown it with the people who care most about you."

Roger thought of his own son, who had graduated from college, started in his career, and married a lovely, intelligent young woman. But what if it had been otherwise? What would he and his wife do if they were the ones who had received a letter giving them the choice: a yellow ribbon, or, if you prefer, I'll go on and leave you alone?

"Norman," he said, "I'm sure you are becoming more nervous and afraid the closer we come to Bennington. But we have to look for that yellow ribbon. Would you like for me to look for you, and let you know?"

"Oh, if you would, I would appreciate it," responded Norman. "Maybe we should even tell the driver to slow down a bit there."

After they had told the driver of the situation, Norman did not care that front seat passengers had overheard, and soon everyone on the bus was aware of it, all assuring him that they would watch

When the bus slowed down at the edge of Bennington, Norman and Roger were back in their seat, Norman with his head bowed and his eyes covered. All at once, Norman heard a loud cheer from everyone on the bus. Roger was clasping his shoulder and saying, "Norman, look up! Look now!"

Norman raised his head and looked out the window. The oak tree was decorated with yellow ribbons, from the top branch to the lowest branch.

GREAT NEWS!
WE'LL CELEBRATE!

Ruth Perry hurried toward the phone, a letter in her hand. The mail had brought something so important that she couldn't wait for her husband to get home. She would call him at work. The letter was that important. She punched the number.

"Dan! I had to call you right away! You won't believe the news! It's a letter from Norman!"

"Yes, after five years of hearing nothing, our son has written us. He's coming Saturday."

"Dan, the letter is postmarked from Cessna, and you know what's there: the prison. That's where he's been."

"Yes, I wish he had let us know a lot sooner, too. It seems he went to Rittenburg, but fell in with a bad crowd who robbed and extorted. They all got arrested before long, and Norman also did five years time. He's due to be released now, and his plan is to get on a bus in this direction."

"But Dan, he's not assuming that we even want to see him. He says he would like to come home for a little while and get his life going right. For sure, he says he has learned some important things and wants to pick up his life and be productive. He says if we will simply tie a yellow ribbon on a lower branch of that oak tree which can be seen from the road, he will get off the bus at Bennington and come home. The bus comes to Bennington about 3:00 in the afternoon. If he doesn't see the ribbon, he will go on."

"Alright, I'll read you the letter:"

"Dear Mom and Dad:

You'll be shocked to hear from me, I know. I hadn't treated you very well and couldn't wait to get away. I went to Rittenberg, but ended up in the prison at Cessna. I joined in with some fellows who were about as arrogant and stupid as I was at the time. We robbed and extorted, and one day got busted. I got five years. It's not pleasant, but I learned some things and also had time to think. I'm due to be released Saturday, the 25th, and I'll take a bus in the direction of home. Now, I would not blame you if you want nothing more to do with me. I'm really sorry for the pain I've caused. I know I blew it big time. But I really want to get busy, work, and learn more, and amount to something. If you're willing to have me at home for a little while, just tie a yellow ribbon on a lower limb of that oak tree at the edge of the property, so that I can see it from the road as the bus goes by. Then I'll get off at Bennington. If I don't see the yellow ribbon, I'll simply stay on the bus. Maybe I can find some place to stay at Victor City and maybe someone will give me work. I don't know how it will turn out. Anyway, now you know what happened with me. And I'm coming nearby.

Love,

Norman"

"So that's the letter, Dan."

"Dan, I haven't heard you cry in a long time."

"Yes, we ought to celebrate. I've no objection to having a party, using the fine special dishes, and breaking out the stuff that we've kept for a special occasion. But remember, Dan, that's not what he's asking. All he's asking for is that yellow ribbon."

"That's right; that's the first thing we've got to do. I'll find a couple of rolls of yellow ribbon, cut the pieces, and when you get home we'll get our ladders and decorate the tree! Hurry home, dear!"

RIVER OF LIFE

Glacier of spirit,
warmed by divine breath,
streamlets of hope,
running with joy,
conquering rocks of despair,
yielding power from dams of disappointment
leaping on past grove and shadow,
carrying comfort by boat and barge,
finds at last the sea of fulfillment.

WAXING WANING MOON

A glimmering curve of light
on the path of heaven
shows hope anew of comfort,
peace, and grace,
filling more each night until
the brightness shows full face.
Slowly the rays are dimmed,
calming by degrees each night
until at last the quiet peace
of joys remembered, grace attained
and hope fulfilled bids the curve
of light farewell until once more regained.

HAIKU REVERIE

Comfort in the rain
comes as a beloved's voice
and rainbow of hope.

Gentle strains of harp
sway with clear haunting flute notes
to murmur deep peace.

Scent of candle sooths
the spirit as memory
of joyous repasts.

TO DANCE

The mirth amid
the weal,
the gratitude amid
the taken for granted
come as fruits of joy,
and set the feet
upon a rhythmic shimmering orb
to balance pain and fear.

ON THE PATH

A year brings seasons,
hope, and challenges, gain and loss.
Take the hope and build
your plans and goals
to share your joy.
Take the challenges
and fear them not,
for they can build a character of worth.
With loss and pain resolve
to build a greater good
for those whose paths are steep.

LIFE AND VICTORY

Another year of life, of hope, of song,
and some I've known who did not have as long
to meet the challenges and drink the joys
of knowing nature's beauty and man's noise.
To each is given bane and burdens, though
with talents we may strive and come to know
those victories which overcome the grief
and bring to others hope and sweet relief.
As victim one may languish in a state
of hopeless melancholy, cursing fate.
To be a victor means a strength to hold
to power above the self, becoming bold
to comfort others with a quiet peace
and love which causes pain of grief to cease.

SPRING BLESSINGS

Aha! I saw some daffodils today.
Spring's lovely heralds have arrived to say
"Our sunshine is for you, despite the rain;
think now on many blessings you can gain."
Lighthearted I went on to face my tasks
and give them my best efforts; he who asks
the reason for the sunshine on my face
will hear of hope and love and awesome grace.
Though rain may fall today, spring still is here,
and moments with my loved ones near and dear
are touched with hope and brightness with a grace
that glides into the summer days apace.
Through rain and sunshine I have learned to see
the blessings large and small surrounding me.

WHAT MATTERS

Of wealth I may have little;
my features may be plain.
My learning may be limited;
from humans comes disdain.
But there is one to whom I'm queen,
because I feed and care for her.
She feels my love, my feline pet,
a comfort with her peaceful purr.

CINQUAIN CREATURES

Feline
with stealthy feet
finding me in my chair
purring to settle on my lap
content.

Canine
whose eyes are bright
with tail atwirl and high
with feet pattering on the floor
dances.

Rabbit
soft and bashful,
twitching nose, floppy ears,
hopping in the grass and flowers,
smooth coat.

CONTENTMENT

My needs are met, though hopes are present still.
Peace is in the heart, come either thrill or chill.
With cherished ones I share life's puzzling way
and meet together each unfolding day.
Living free from envy of those blessed in other ways
is knowing my own gifts for present days.
Living free from bitterness for all past wrongs to me,
and living as forgiven for pain I've caused, I see
contentment which is as a fruitful tree.

THE RACE

Let me be ten seconds
in a well run race
rather than a wasted day,
so that when He comes
walking in the garden
I don't have to hide.

HAIKU GEMS

Garnets and rubies
delight a soul with valor
and shine as new wine.

Sapphires with beauty
of phlox and sky and ocean
reflect a peace of soul.

Emeralds do shine
for life and youth and trust
'mid forests of calm.

Topaz of sunshine
sparkles as golden cider
in refreshing joy.

MIND

Made to observe the vastness of our world,
the greater breadth and depth of stars unfurled,
the mind can grasp an order and a plan
and ponder the deep question, "Who is man?"
To cherish all the power of lovely thought
so that it builds up courage as it ought
is to expand my joy when joy I share
and blessings pass to all on earth so fair.
If I can mirror compassion, love, and grace
'twill be a beacon to us in the race
wherein we seek a good and lasting goal:
to show the treasures given to the soul.
Alas, some minds in frightening darkness writhe
And grasp no order, though they are alive.

BERLIN

A city sundered by a wall of might
where one half writhes beneath a cruel yoke
and one half thrives on freedom for its folk
cannot remain asunder with continued night.

'Twas war that brought about the breach of trust
when victors came to draw another map,
and one would force a tyranny and wrap
one section under despots' rule unjust.

I stood at twenty-five and viewed the wall
with wreaths for those who did not live to see
the day of hope; yet would I live to be
a witness when the cruel stones would fall?

With not yet fifty years I watched the dance
of joy as answered prayers gave right a chance.

REMEMBER THE COST

Freedom has an awful cost
in blood and grief and pain.
Stand strong, and let it not be lost
in callousness and pursuits vain.
Remember those who gave their all
that tyranny should not prevail,
and those who live with wounds behind a wall
and ask if they did strive to no avail.
To cherish liberty aright
in gratitude for those who paid the price
is to be free to bear the light
to those who follow: heed the sage advice.

CRIME VICTIM

Could I have been there
as you cried in pain
I would have cried for magic powers
to thwart the thugs and set you free.
From where I am, I'll raise my prayers
for justice and your healing.
God grieves for you and your tormentors,
lost in darkness, bondage, sin.
I pray for light, for reason, peace within.

THERAPY

My fingers dance as notes swell from the heart.
The strains of joy rise to delight the ear
of one who loves the ancient form of art,
language universal, eloquent, clear.

In song I find a fount of hope and grace,
and faith that comforts in the midst of care;
encouragement for trials I must face,
and blessings which will echo far from there.

Melody in playing my own feeling
lifts my spirit's heavy burdens pressing.
Joy deepens with bright hopes appealing,
manifest in very richest blessing.

As strength and healing come to one in pain
So music comes as rainbow through the rain.

WOUNDED DOVE

Hate is a destructive power
against the hater most of all.
Its target's pain comes hour by hour,
but torment on the hater will fall.
Forgiveness is the target's choice
to embrace a healing reason 'twined with love.
Oh, world, awake and hear blest reason's voice.
Leave off the violence; nurse the wounded dove
and know that hate must die,
and life and triumph with God lie.

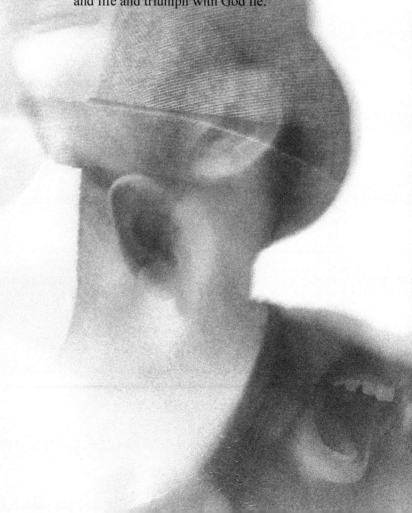

PEACE

No war, no fear of an impending strife,
or is it fragile truce across a line?
The heart of man can hate e'en one's own life
with even less regard for yours or mine.
To be just left alone to do my thing
and live unhindered as I hone my thought
may give me fleeting peace to work or sing,
yet in a while I still may find a draught.
Where is the peace which does not come from chance,
but springs within and soothes the stress without?
By it the heart can conquer circumstance
and sing with hope amid the waves of doubt.
To man this peace was promised and assured
for those who look above, and have endured.

GRACE

Mercy from a bigger heart than mine,
forbearance from a love which fears not pain,
peace which rises as a steadfast sign
of infinite compassion, awesome gain:
all this brings tears of joy abounding
and awesome hope and trust in One so great
Who still with me His grace surrounding
leads me where blessings greater still await.

FLORAL CINQUAINS

Tulips
Pink in freshness
Red and white in sweetness
Yellow in a glow of good cheer
Dancing

Roses
Red for heartstrings
White and pure for newness
Yellow in the sun at noontime
Lovely

Lilacs
Deepest purple
Pale lavender and white
May's fairest blossoms on the tree
Fragrant

Lilies
White and regal
In splendor and glory
Clothed richly as the greatest king
Alive

Iris
Shades of purple
Yellow, beige and ermine
Enthralling the eye and the heart
Noble

STORM

Shall the tempest me affright
when it drenches all in sight?
Shall the tempest yet prevail
with its rain and chilling hail?
Lightening rends the sulking cloud
which roars again with thunder proud.
Torrent turns to gentle mist
and by its touch the earth is kissed.
The tempest's tantrum soon is spent
and leaves the day with breeze content.
Lightening need not rend the sky.
The sun and moon are firm and high
illumining a landscape now at peace,
for God can bid a storm be still and cease.

STRUGGLE

Too little, and it seems so much to pay.
Indeed, I do hope for a better day.
I juggle numbers, practicing my math,
thinking hard to find an easier path.
Work and toil, needs and wants, and cares of life,
with gold and silver bound, and fraud is rife.
I'll pray for wisdom and an honest heart,
and add contentment for my every part.

CHOOSE LIFE

Choose reason, for it is a gift
to humankind alone to stand in awe
of that vast order from the stars to tiny flowers.
Choose to grow in mercy and in strength
of character and courage to pursue the right,
though it may cost your day's best hours.
Choose life and all it brings
of blessing, challenge, gain and loss,
that God may teach you through His powers.

LET'S REBUILD!

It wasn't as though the townspeople of Perrysville didn't care. Indeed, they were a close knit community. They had, for one thing, the Clayton Center to which a number of children through the years had come for help in times of crisis, for a comforting mentor to help them pick up the pieces after a life-changing event such as parents' divorce or even the death of a family member. Others came simply for attention and friendship when parents' lives became too busy and complicated. Then one night a fire destroyed the Clayton Center.

"We will have to rebuild it," said Benjamin Wells, an active and prominent attorney. "We will need people who can give not only money, but the time and effort which it takes for such a project. There are some adults in this town who spent time there as children. I hope they will think about what it did for them, and how they could give something back now."

Larry Skyles, his partner in the firm, nodded. "My father died when I was twelve," he answered. "I found some friends there who really cared about me. Even though they could not bring back my father, I knew that I was not alone as I faced growing up."

"Your story of losing your father is not uncommon, Larry," replied Mr. Wells. "It's a world where tragedies happen. The key is that people recover by focusing on others, or on the common good."

"I believe that's true," responded Mr. Skyles. "In my case, I had my mother who was left alone with my sister Susan and me. Susan also had lost a good father, and my mother would never have expected that a heart attack would leave her a widow when her children were twelve and ten. First of all the three of us had to sit down with each other and decide how to do everything at home with three people instead of four. I think that was probably the easiest part. The hardest part was missing a person who could not be replaced."

"It's important not to feel alone," added Ben. "That meant people had to put themselves aside and focus on you. Now, here in Perrysville we have people who will focus on others' needs rather than themselves. We need to see somehow that they are approached and made aware of what they can do."

"Some will be able to do more than others," replied Larry. "But each needs to feel that his or her contribution is important. That's what then leads to the willingness to give of oneself, whether of money, time, or skill."

"Larry, do you think that it's easier to ask people for money, or for time?" asked Ben.

"That's an interesting question," answered Larry. "I've done both. People do not have equal amounts of money, of course. But everyone has twenty-four hours each day, seven days each week. Yet, they say that when you want something done, ask a busy person. It's true. The busy person knows how to make efficient use of time."

"Do you know Lillian Burgess?" asked Ben. "She's a special education teacher with a lot of responsibilities, but she gets things done. She might have some good ideas about whom to approach and how to get the ball rolling for the Clayton Center."

"I've met her several times," replied Larry. "My nephew Allen is in one of her classes, and he seems to really like her. I'll try to call her tonight."

Lillian Burgess was happy to talk with Larry Skyles and get right down to the essentials. "I'll go to the bank tomorrow to open an account for the rebuilding fund," she said. "The first deposit will be my contribution. Then, we will need to make the public aware of the fund."

"So won't that mean the radio and TV stations, and the newspaper?" asked Larry. "How much are we looking at?"

"A considerable sum," answered Lillian. "I will make some phone calls and get some precise numbers. But perhaps we should first approach some churches and service organizations to make inexpensive announcements to their membership. A number of those people, each putting in even a modest amount, could raise enough money for the ads, and a good amount toward the construction."

"Then we'll need a few persons who are good at designing ads," added Larry. "They will be asked for their time. Surely, they are out there and would do it."

"I know a graphic designer whom I could ask, and I can think of two or three people to approach about media ads," replied Lillian thoughtfully. "Once all that is in place, we will come to the nitty gritty. By that I mean individuals and how much they would give of either time or money."

"Can you explain the project to the faculty at your school, and incidentally at a PTA meeting?" suggested Larry.

"Oh, yes, I'll do that," responded Lillian. "That's using the inexpensive, word-of-mouth method first. Moreover, I'll also make it known to the congregation at my church."

"Definitely," replied Larry. "And while I'm talking to my pastor about it, I'll ask him whether he would bring it up at the next pastors' meeting. That would spread the word through several churches. I think we are on our way!"

A week had passed. The second contribution to the bank account for the Clayton Center was from the Wells & Skyles law firm. During the weeks after that, other donations came in to build up the fund. Then, an attractive full page ad ran in the Perrysville Gazette. And several people had come forward to call their friends and neighbors to encourage them to help. These people reported various responses, from "Well, my husband simply can't see giving money away," to "We don't really need to spend money for that weekend outing; this is more important." One family had planned a garage sale. Now, the proceeds would go to the Clayton Center fund. Others said, "I wish it could be more, but I hope this will help."

Over the next month, the fund grew from contributions large and small. But those who had the most exciting time were the children in Lillian Burgess' class. "Can we do something?" they had asked. "Can we make things to sell? Can we do jobs for people? Could we even do a talent show?" Obviously, their wheels were turning, and they were willing to be generous with their time. The plan came into place as Lillian Burgess listened to and directed the ideas. They would schedule an evening for a talent show, combined with a silent auction of things which the children had made or brought. There were baked items, toys, needlework, pictures, plants, and other things.

Some students who did jobs such as caring for pets, cleaning, or lawn mowing, would put their next jobs' earnings into the fund raised by Lillian Burgess' class.

Finally the big evening came. Many people came, ready for an evening of fun.

Allen Danforth was known as a shy lad who was nevertheless intelligent. He had simply had the misfortune to be crippled in an accident. He had helped his teacher with fliers and invitations, but wished that he could do more. He had brought to the auction a small box of pins, figurines, pictures, and decorative items. They had been his treasured keepsakes. They sold for enough to buy several attractive and therapeutic toys at the rebuilt Clayton Center.

When the new center was dedicated, Larry Skyles called Allen Danforth forward to thank him for his part. "You gave what you could, and more," he said. "And good things have come out of an unfortunate loss. You are an important part of it, and we're proud of you."

The applause which followed told Allen that even small acts of selflessness count for much.